Y0-DYH-433

Home Less In Dallas

Troy Harris II

Copyright © 2023 by Troy Harris II.

All rights reserved. This book is a work of fiction. Names, characters, and incidents either are products of the author's imagination or are used fictitiously.

No part of this book may be reproduced in any written, electronic, or recorded form or photocopied without written permission from the publisher or author. If you would like permission to use material from the book (other than for review purposes), please contact the author or publisher. Thank you for your support of the author's rights.

To purchase books in bulk or for additional information, contact the publisher.

Mynd Matters Publishing
715 Peachtree Street NE
Suites 100 & 200
Atlanta, GA 30308
www.myndmatterspublishing.com

ISBN: 978-1-957092-65-2 (pbk)
ISBN: 978-1-957092-66-9 (hdcv)

FIRST EDITION

Dedication

For Eli.

With fond love for Aidan, Blake, Marcus, and Remy.

Written to anyone out there trying to make something of themselves, as I was these handful of months. May you build promising relationships, feed those ideas, and make ends meet. I encourage you to chase that dream, even if it's a little too big for you right now, because you never know what's waiting on you just up the street.

Table of Contents

Foreword

Look up the name Troy, and you'll find that its most common definition is "footsoldier." Of course, it is related to the ancient Greek city of Troy, however, when I think about Troy Harris, the name still remains the same.

A soldier is a person who served in the army, and Troy is a person who serves. In the process of learning deeper service, particularly the service to humanity, to community, to God, and to family, I've seen a few of the ups and downs that Troy has experienced, and they were all working together for his good, and therefore *our* collective good.

I've had the pleasure of knowing Troy as a participant in my nonprofits career training program, and as a member of our extended family in my hometown of Dallas, and now in Atlanta, where my sister resides.

Home is not just where the heart is, but it is also where you connect with the hearts of others, be it over a meal or over a matter. I can recall true heart to heart conversations with Troy about the vicissitudes of life and how as a family and a generation, we would make it through. I can also recall the laughter of the conversations he and my dad have had, and the joy of the collaboration that he and my sister, Savannah, make in her greeting card line. Family. Real family.

The good thing about family, especially the ones you like, is that you don't have to talk to them all of the time to feel their spirit and their love. Now, as Troy creates his own family, he extends the branches to the tree of our common good and common humanity.

I celebrate the work that he is doing, and trust that you will find his story inspiring.

LINCOLN CHRISTOPHER STEPHENS
Social Entrepreneur, Co-Founder of the Marcus Graham Project

Preface

This book is largely an account of me trying to make sense of where I was then. Chasing the dream of becoming a writer, the benefits of building an invaluable network, and the thrill of one day owning a business. I was looking for success in all the funky ways it decided to present itself.

During this time, I only knew two things: I was uncomfortable, and I was in what seemed like a truly foreign land.

As it turns out, I was just home less in Dallas.

Hundreds of miles away, and almost ten years later, here are some of those strange times that I'll never forget.

Home Less In Dallas (Intro)

...because I was

Home Less In Dallas

I used to be homeless in Dallas. Yeah, seriously. It was tough, but it was fun. It taught me a lot about a lot, but mostly it was just hot. I mean, it *is* Texas after all.

But after the summer, it got extremely cold. There was an ice storm and everything! I bet you didn't know that about Dallas, did you? Yeah, that was news to me, too. I didn't even come with a coat.

Any-who, that's one of the many little things about being homeless. You spend so much time getting close to things you never noticed before — like the patterns of the sun (and the shade), or which train stops have public bathrooms, and which McDonald's has the hottest fries. Your antennas are always up, because they have to be — you're homeless.

Now, by homeless in Dallas, I just mean that I didn't have a place in the city to call my own. Though, I spent many days roaming the streets at odd hours of the night, thankfully, there were couches, and empty offices, and cars, and friends' floors, and even some beds along the way that got the job done. So to say "homeless" would be a bit heavy-handed, I suppose. Let's just say I was home...less.

Whew...now, where was I? Oh yeah—learning.

As a home less person in Dallas, I learned a lot about a lot.

I learned lessons in friendship and leadership, opportunity and perspective. I honed my cooking skills and my character. I learned how to spot a rye from a bourbon, celebrated my first Juneteenth, went from no job to two jobs in one weekend, and even got my ass kicked in dominoes. It was, in many accounts, a second childhood for me. A childhood void of a home, but somehow cozy nonetheless.

It showed me that both success and failure are truly imposters, and that earning your stripes is even harder to do when you have nothing to lose.

I learned that most of the skills we *really* need in life — like kindness, curiosity, and always trying your best — we probably learned way back in kindergarten.

I saw just how far a question like, *"Would you like half of my sandwich?"* can take a relationship and the many ways you can make use of a big red couch.

Oh, and I wasn't alone either — all of my friends were home less too! You'll learn more about them later; I have a bunch of stories. However, the moral of *this* story is that being home less in Dallas isn't much different than *not* being home less in Dallas, or any other city for that matter. In some ways, we're all constantly searching for home, whether we realize it or not.

Adversity is everywhere, and it's when the stakes are the highest that your truest self shines the brightest.

So, with that said, here come the fables. Some are fast and others are funny. Some are informative and some are inspirational. But most of them are just flat out weird.

Because being home *less* is weird...especially in Dallas. You'll see.

Eat Your Burger, Drink Your Beer

...because time is precious

I used to be home *less* in Dallas. And by home *less*, I mean that I simply did not have one. This was my life, and to say that it taught me a lot about a lot would be a grave understatement—but I said it anyway, at the beginning of the first chapter.

All these years later, I still vividly remember what it taught me about staying in the moment, and putting first things first:

It taught me how to eat my burger, and drink my beer.

Look, when you're home less, there are few more important ways to spend the little money you *do* have than on food. I mean, it's not like you have rent to pay. So, when I walked into that random Dallas burger bar, on that random afternoon that summer, it instantly became a home for me and my crew.

Now, there are many things I could tell you about this crew, but I suppose the most important thing here is that we were close. They were my business partners, my friends, and most of them were home less too; which is to say that we spent many hours of many days together. And on this particular day, our plan was to spend our time together, enjoying this meal.

We got comfortable, each ordered a burger and a beer, and started chit-chatting—per usual.

I think it was a conspiracy theory about the moon landing...or maybe politics...or Chinese horoscopes...or new music (or maybe old music)...or something. You know, whatever home less folks talk about in the middle of the day, in the middle of Dallas burger bars.

Whatever it was, though, it got deep. That's for sure.

And, unsurprisingly, before long we were fully invested in yelling at each other. Pointing fingers, clapping hands, trying to make our points over raised voices. It was sort of intense. Loud. This wasn't new for us—like I said, we were close—but it was probably the wrong place at the wrong time, now that I think about it.

The waiter brought the beers out, and we kept talking. Several minutes later, the burgers came out, and yet, still we continued this albatross of a convo. If you'd have been there that day, you probably would've thought we weren't even thirsty or hungry, which obviously wasn't true because we were *always* thirsty and hungry. But all we seemed to be interested in was yelling back and forth at each other.

Well, somewhere between the ill-effects of a bicameral legislature, and the year of the Rat, my burger got cold and my beer got warm. Not good. I missed my window to enjoy what *should* have been the best part of my day. I'd failed to put first things first. We all did.

Now, it is not lost on me how interesting this conversation must've been for us home less (and hungry) people to neglect our food like we did, but we damn sure did. And yeah, I'm sure quality ideas were swapped and perspectives were exchanged, but my biggest takeaway has nothing to do with the conversation at all.

In fact, as I sit here thinking back on it, I can't even remember what we were talking about, who all was there, or the name of the restaurant. The only thing that's stuck in my head all these years later, is that cold burger and that warm ass beer! That's it.

And see, that's the thing about life, whether you're home less in Dallas or not. Moments are precious, which is why we're taught to put first things first. It's a cliche for a reason.

Sometimes, living in the moment places competing priorities in front of us, and it's not always cut and dry which should come first.

And, in that regard, being home less is no different than not being home less; it takes focus. It's equal parts science and art—and in this case, I should have struck while the burger was hot...and the beer was cold. Instead, we wanted so badly to be heard (and "right") that we ruined what was right in front of us.

As it turns out, being home less and having an ego are *not* mutually exclusive.

I learned to eat my burger and drink my beer, not only on the off chance that I don't know where my next meal is coming from, but because it's important to tackle what's on your plate before worrying about something else.

I learned to eat my burger and drink my beer, not because I'm afraid to waste my food, but because I'm afraid to waste the moment.

I learned to eat my burger and drink my beer because time is precious, and it shouldn't take being home less to live in that truth.

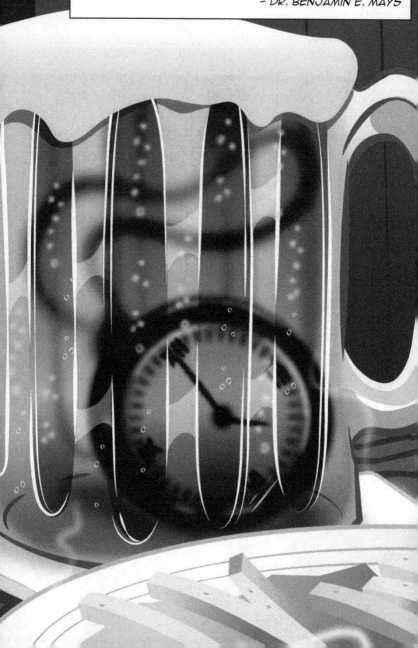

"I HAVE ONLY JUST A MINUTE, ONLY SIXTY SECONDS IN IT. FORCED UPON ME, CAN'T REFUSE IT. DIDN'T SEEK IT, DIDN'T CHOOSE IT. BUT IT'S UP TO ME TO USE IT. I MUST SUFFER IF I LOSE IT. GIVE ACCOUNT IF I ABUSE IT. JUST A TINY LITTLE MINUTE, BUT ETERNITY IS IN IT."

– DR. BENJAMIN E. MAYS

The Big Red Couch

...because sharing is caring

I used to sleep on a big red couch.

Well, it wasn't all that big, but it was *definitely* red as hell. Especially when the light hit it just right during the day time. I remember it well. It was one of those shiny couches that made noise when you moved around on it. Kinda fancy, sort of chic, and definitely made more for sitting than sleeping, that's for sure. But I slept on it. We all did.

Now, that's not to say the couch didn't get sat on every day. A lot of times by me and the crew, and a lot of times by other folks too. Friends, family, rich folks, drunk folks, Black folks, all types of folks. It was a damn good couch.

It was shaped in this inviting sorta way that made the people sitting on it want to talk to each other. It also formed a semi-circle around this matching ottoman type of piece that sat in the middle of everything. The ottoman was definitely for your feet, but most people sat on it so they could chat with the rest of the couch.

... but when everyone was gone, we slept on that shit too! That's just how we got down.

This big red couch was in a multi-use industrial office just south of downtown, and owned by a friend and mentor of ours. We'd managed to get the key from him one way or another for some one-off thing, and he never quite got around to asking for it back. So, we started to live there. Don't ask, don't tell.

See, that's the thing about being home less: sometimes you fancy forgiveness over permission.

I even made love on that couch once. Well, I wouldn't quite call it *love* because there wasn't anything too special about what went down that afternoon, and it didn't really take us all that long either (cringe), but I sure did love *whatever* it was we did on that couch a lot more than I did sleeping on it.

Anyway, it was a one-time thing that I never told the other fellas about. Besides, something tells me there are quite a few things I didn't know about that big red couch. It was just that kind of couch.

So, what I'm saying is that the couch was a lot of things to a lot of people. Office adornment by day, bed by night, and whatever the hell else in between. And you better believe we shared it like our lives depended on it. Primarily because our lives did depend on it.

And while we're on the topic of sharing, the best part of the couch was this blanket on it. Now, when I say blanket, I really mean a throw, and by throw, I'm just saying it wasn't all that big.

So yeah, it was *just* about long enough to stretch from your shoulders to your knees, and wide enough to barely wrap under your butt on both sides. It was a one-man-show, point, blank, period. Keep in mind, this couch and blanket were in this industrial building I was telling you about— surrounded by concrete, exposed brick, and hardwood — and it sat right by a floor-to-ceiling window that always carried a draft with it. Look, if no one has told you that it's not always warm in Dallas, let me be the first. It got chilly at night time, and that blanket came in handy.

Let me paint the picture for you. You may go your whole life and not see this small of a blanket play such a huge role in someone's life - home less or not.

The four of us took turns with the blanket, and, naturally, rotated it every four days. This went on for weeks: waiting until your Blanket Day came, stretching it from your shoulders to your knees, tucking it under your butt *just* so, and fetching some sleep.

Then...you'd wake up, pass it to the next man, and wait again. It was the perfect solution to our imperfect predicament. That might sound sad or boring, but here's how it taught me virtue.

I remember once in the late Fall, it had been pretty cold all week. I'd anxiously awaited my Blanket Day, and when it finally came (it must've been a Thursday), it had the nerve to be warm as hell outdoors! I woke up the next morning with it kicked all over the floor. I hadn't needed it.

"It was just my luck to have a warm night on *my* turn to use the blanket," I thought to myself. But fair is fair (is it really?), and that was *my* Blanket Day.

Well, as fate would have it, the very next night was chilly again, and I was three days in the hole, freezing my ass off. I guess Mother Nature really does have a mind of her own.

My first instinct was to petition that I hadn't even used it the night before, with it being so hot, and ask for it back. "It be like that sometimes," the dude with the blanket told me as he dozed off.

I sat in silence for some minutes before eventually shrugging it off, and shivering my ass to sleep. I'd learned the golden rule in kindergarten, and now it was time to put it to use. Tough, but fair. Simple, but not easy. It was *his* blanket.

And that's something about being home less in Dallas that maybe isn't specific to being home less, or being in Dallas at all. Sharing is caring, bruh, and fair is fair. Whether it's a friend, a business partner, or just another person that inhabits your situation (this crew of mine fell into all three categories), mutual respect and dependability go a long way in life.

And you know what? So does appreciation. Because no matter the cards we're dealt, knowing how *not* to take the little things (like tiny blankets) for granted is a muscle that needs to be exercised in order for it to stay strong (no matter the weather).

Dependability. Appreciation. Patience. These are the virtues we were being force fed in a cold, stolen office, sleeping on a not-so-big red couch with four other grown men. They are virtues that we wound up having to learn the hard way. Virtues that I won't ever have to learn again, trust me.

Eventually, we were kicked out of that office... and off of that couch. Nothing lasts forever, I'm told. The day had finally come where we'd wake up, fold the blanket, and place it back on that center ottoman for the final time. It was time to go and be home less somewhere else in Dallas. I'll tell you more about that another time.

For now, just know that the Big Red Couch was more than just a big red couch. It was a microcosm of the larger landscape of life. A not-so-gentle reminder that no man is an island, and that everybody has a little light under the sun.

Can you dig that?

I'LL LEAVE YOU WITH SOMETHING MY BARBER ALWAYS TELLS ME:

"ONE DAY, COFFEE, NEXT DAY, TEA. TODAY IT'S YOU, TOMORROW IT'S ME."

The Black Peacoat (Skit)

...because Mama knows best

The Black Peacoat (skit)

A quick, spirited phone conversation between a son chasing a dream in a new place, and a tough-loving mother who'd rather him simply come home.

Troy: Hey Ma, what's up?

Mama: Hi Son, how are you?

Troy: I'm okay, you?

Mama: Fine.... You okay?

Troy: Hmmm... Why wouldn't I be?

Mama: Did you just answer my question with a question?

Troy: Can we start over?

Mama: You must want something?

Troy: Want something? Hmmmm?

Mama: Hello?! What is it?

Troy: Can I have some money, Ma?

Mama: Money?

Troy: Please?

Mama: For what?

Troy: Little of this and that, you know?

Mama: You sound skinny, are you eating?

Troy: How come you can answer my questions with a quest... nevermind. Now, when you say *eating*... what do you mean, exactly?

Mama: When are you coming home?

Troy: I have a home here, remember?

Mama: Do you?

Troy: Hmmm?

Mama: Hello?!

Troy: Can I have some money, Ma? Please?

Mama: What's that noise?

Troy: What noise?

Home Less In Dallas

Mama: *Are you outside?*

Troy: Yes... why?

Mama: *Sounds cold there. Is that the wind?*

Troy: The wind?

Mama: *The wind. Do you even have a coat?*

Troy: Mom, I'm hungry. Can we talk about that?

Mama: *Are you near a Target?*

Troy: Yes, why?

Mama: *Black or Brown?*

Troy: Huh?

Mama: *Do you want a black or brown peacoat?*

Troy: Can we maybe talk about black and brown beans instead?

Mama: *I'm online now, did you hear me?*

Troy: Hmmmm?

Mama: *Hello?!*

Troy: Uhhh... do they have black in my size?

Mama: *Can you pick it up today?*

Troy: But what about money for some food?

Mama: I'm cooking in Atlanta for Christmas, will I see you then?

Troy: Idk. Thanksgiving hasn't even come, has it?

Mama: Is that your way of saying no?

Troy: No, but can I have some food money?

Mama: Hmmmm?

Troy: Hello?

Mama: Let me know how the jacket fits. I love you, Son. Bye!

Damn, it's cold out here.

"DAMN IT'S COLD OUT HERE."

Throwing
D. A. R. T. S.

...because you're not always lucky

Home Less In Dallas

Ok, so not only did I not have a place to live, I didn't have a car. Sad story, I know. This was made alright, however, by a few things.

First off, I didn't mind walking. Yeah, it sucked sometimes, but there are worse things in the world, and I understood that. More times than not, I was more than okay to "pick 'em up, and put 'em down" until I got wherever it was that I was going.

Secondly, there was this bike that sort of... existed outside of the office that contained the Big Red Couch. We didn't know whose bike it was, but I'm sure some people thought it was mine as much as I rode it. It was perfect for late night Taco Bell runs, or to just go find a mid-morning breeze when you didn't have shit else to do.

However, the most important asset (by far) to me not having a car, was the Dallas Area Rapid Transit metro system, or the DART.

It was the public train that went all over the city, and got me through every journey not fit to walk or bike to. At the time, ridesharing was still mostly for black car services, and not nearly as "everywhere" as it is now, so that wasn't an option—not that I could afford it anyway. Hell, I couldn't even afford to ride the damn DART itself!

Which actually brings me to the whole point of this story.

The DART was dope because it operated on an honor system. And the honorable thing to do was to pay to ride it. There were no ticket counters underground like in New York City. No turnstiles, no scanning or checking before walking on, no nothing. To this day, the trains just sit above ground, and are easily accessible to the street... but the unwritten rule was to visit the machine and get a ticket before boarding.

Ok, I lied, it wasn't unwritten. It was actually *very clearly* written on signs all around at every stop: "RIDING THIS TRAIN WITHOUT A TICKET IS ILLEGAL. VIOLATORS WILL BE PROSECUTED!"

Eh, don't quote me, but it probably said something like that.

Yeahhhh..... I'm quite sure that I don't have to tell you this, but I never paid for a ticket. Like ever. I knew what the honorable thing to do was, but there's no honor amongst thieves, and, well, part of being home less is sometimes being a thief.

"The DART was practically made for poor, home less, people like me, right?!" is what I'd tell myself. Whether right or wrong, I figured The Universe would understand. I wasn't robbing Peter to pay Paul. I was robbing both. My hands were tied. What did they want from me? Exactly.

And, sure enough, The Universe seemed to understand. No matter how many times I turned blind eyes and deaf ears to the posted signs and loudspeaker announcements instructing me to do the right thing, I was spared. Sure, if I was caught, the consequence was a monetary fine, but seeing as though I couldn't even afford a ticket in the first place... that reality never, ever landed.

Sometimes being home less means being too broke to be afraid.

I spent many days taking whatever ride I needed, to get wherever I was going, and was never caught. I'd ride all over the city to meetings, or to the mall, to parties me and the boys would sneak into, wherever — scot-free. Some would call us lucky, I'd just call us broke.

But mostly lucky.

Well, at a certain point, I got a job. A couple jobs actually. Just some little part-time gigs. One at the restaurant across the street, and another helping out around the office. No car (or home), but I had some pocket change and that was a good thing. Still though, the DART was my best friend. And that's where this gets interesting.

Over the previous months, I'd become so accustomed to not paying to ride when I *didn't* have a job, that I refused to start buying tickets once I *did* have one. I called myself being fiscally smart, but really I was just being reckless.

The compassion The Universe had granted me for being poor would soon disappear when I started to be greedy.

I know this because not even a week after I'd gotten the job, I saw my first cop checking passengers' tickets on the train in between stops. I didn't have a ticket (I never had one) but managed to sneak off that bad boy...barely. It was the first time I had ever even come close to getting caught. Something had shifted around me, I could feel it.

Now, most people would have taken that as a sign to start paying, seeing as though I technically could now, but you wouldn't be reading this story if I had done that, would you?

Sure enough, within a couple of days, I was caught ticket-less and fined $50. I was hit. Bullseye.

With power (my little part-time jobs) came the responsibility to do the right thing (buying a $2 DART ticket), and I didn't. I guess I turned a blind eye and a deaf ear to that part too.

There is something to be learned here because even as a struggling home less person in Dallas, I was taken care of. Whether it was an unexpected meal, a place to lay my head for a night, or a safe ride on the DART that I couldn't afford, my needs were met. The Universe respects need and intention.

It wasn't until I was *able* to act honorably and do right financially (and still chose *not* to) that I got "got." I wasn't punished for being poor, I was punished for being greedy. When you know better, you do better. And when you try to hog your gifts, they'll get taken away from you one way or another.

Like I said, it's even harder to earn your stripes when you have nothing to lose.

So, if you ever find yourself in a similar boat, or on a similar train, do the right thing. The first time. Seriously. I'll leave you with this:

"A hard head makes a soft ass." — My Momma

Do The Right Thing!

A D.A.R.T. JOINT

"A HARD HEAD MAKES A SOFT ASS."
— MY MOMMA

Interlude:

Good Day, Bad Day

...because we all have 'em

Home Less In Dallas

I used to work on one side of the street, and it seemed like everyone that I'd meet, in every moment in every way, was having one of their very worst days.

They called the phone to yell in my ear; loud enough for my boss to hear! Looking for this, or looking for that. Demanding I come and pick up their slack.

Well, I didn't like these people, you know? But I was home less with no where to go. And since I had quite a few bigger plans, I just did my job and lent them a hand.

I was working for this property management team; where the perks were never as good as they seemed. Because they would always call me to say, that something was broke on this horrible day.

I used to work on one side of the street, and it seemed like everyone that I'd meet, in every moment in every way, was having one of their very best days.

They'd come, sit down, these women and men; and call me right over to order some gin. Looking to have one hell of a night — yes, indeed a hell of a sight.

Well I grew to like these people, you know? They'd sit there and frolic with nowhere to go. Smiles on their faces and ice in their cup, I'd stand there and smile, and soak it all up.

See, I worked the bar across from those flats. The nights were long, but the tips were fat. So many people to hug and say hey, I'd watch them live out their most perfect days.

And this is how it went for a while. One side fragrant, the other side foul. I started to ponder as I crossed that street, the difference between the people we meet.

Home Less In Dallas

Could it be that some folks have no luck? The ones who catch flus with cars that get stuck? That wake up each day to pain and strife, while some folks have the time of their life.

Plenty of ice cubes with gin in their drink, with nary a worry 'bout clogs in their sink. The folks 'cross the street were just stuck in their tracks, I vowed to leave them and never go back!

I knew the person I'd evolve to be. I hated the bad days, they just weren't for me. I sat at the job that I'd soon leave behind, 'til one day this thought just blew my mind:

I'd just come from lunch a tad bit late, and heard the phone ring as I walked past the slate. This man rambled on and needless to say, before long we were both having a pretty bad day.

His toilet *and* microwave; the A/C again. He even misplaced his recycling bin! I handled his shit and then bid him adieu, then clocked out to clock in at job number 2.

Good times and laughter; happy and gay. Now *these* were the folks that were having a DAY! They were not the type to nag and complain, they just ordered gin; again and again.

But later that evening, who do I see? That "bad-day" fellow, with the broken A/C. Smiling, and grinning, with plenty of friends, he gestured me over and ordered some gin.

BUT LATER THAT EVENING, WHAT DO I SEE? THAT "BAD-DAY" FELLOW, WITH THE BROKEN A/C. SMILES, AND GRINS, WITH PLENTY OF FRIENDS, HE GESTURE ME OVER TO ORDER SOME GIN.

The Texas State Fair

...because everybody is trying to keep the lights on

Home Less In Dallas

You know how they say that everything is bigger in Texas? Right? Right. Well, whoever *they* is... ain't never lied.

If you've ever been to any state fair, you know it's a huge giddy-up. If you've been to the Texas State Fair, in Dallas' Fair Park, you've seen some things. Me? Well, I've never been there. Well, perhaps once but...let's just say that I never made it to the door.

I know what you're thinking, and it's not because I was home less that I didn't make it in. Not this time. To be honest, fairs just weren't ever my thing. Long ATM lines, long lines for subpar food and beverages, and even longer lines to ride the actual rides. It's a whole bunch of "hurry up and wait" that I could simply do without.

So yeah, that's why I've never been to the Texas State Fair. But, I can still tell you all about it. It kept the lights on for us one night.

Ok, so just because *I* wasn't going in, didn't mean that other people weren't. You'd be surprised at how far away people come from once those bright lights come on.

It all boiled down to this: The Fair was a high-dollar event, but the surrounding neighborhood was not. And so, as you can imagine, the locals had the mind to hustle a little bit as out-of-towners, and in-towners alike, poured in with cash to spend. The plan was simple: take advantage of the foot traffic, and make some cold hard cash.

The Fair kicked off, and we observed as people sold t-shirts, peanuts, bottled water, water bottles, umbrellas, hats, umbrella hats, you name it. Whatever they could get their hands on, they set up shop with it, and went to market.

Well, let's just say that after a day or two of watching this whole song-and-dance surrounding The Fair, me and the boys wanted some action. Everybody was selling something, we just needed to create a need. By hook or crook. Build it and they will come, *they* say.

So, whereas some folks might've seen The Fair as a great big display of lights, we saw it as an opportunity to keep our lights on - figuratively of course. And that's exactly what happened on the first day of that weekend.

Let me level with you—sometimes, to succeed in life, you gotta get lucky. And we were lucky. WE knew Mr. Calvin.

Mr. Calvin is a family man, a long-standing deacon in the church, and someone who "never worked for The Man" (let him tell it). The type of cat that's just as much *of* the city as he is *from* the city, and very well integrated into it at that. He knew some of everybody and even co-owned some land about 1/4 mile from the fairgrounds. It was just an old, grassy lot on most weekends, but on Fair Weekend, it transformed into prime real estate, let *us* tell it.

After some prodding, he gifted it to us for the weekend under one condition: "Stay out of trouble, and try and make some damn money." Simple enough.

And just like that, we were in the mix. And while the folks next to us sold t-shirts, peanuts, bottled water, water bottles, umbrellas, hats, umbrella hats, and whatever else they could get their hands on, we sold grass! Well, parking spots on a grassy plot.

I'd be lying if I said we got off to a roaring start. As it turns out, not many people are down to leave their car in a grassy plot with four 20-something-year-old Black dudes waving them down without a sign. And with that said, we struggled mightily for the majority of that Friday afternoon. We lacked whatever it is that makes grassy plots look like parking lots. We weren't official, but thank God, we got lucky again that evening.

It started raining.

There are a lot of things rain can make a man do. But when it comes to The Fair in Texas, turning their car around, and going back home just to stay dry, ain't one of 'em. Now, what these people expected from a wet bag of cotton candy once they got inside had nothing to do with me, but as long as The Fair kept its lights on, we were able to do the same.

And so the rain saved us that night.

How? Simple math. A ¼-mile walk in the rain was a lot less treacherous than the ½-mile or more walk from the other parking lots for sell (even if ours was sketchy, double the price, and not even a "real" parking lot).

You're going to like this next part. We started making money! Hand. Over. Fist. We were playing real-life Tetris with people's vehicles, and we'd turned Mr. Calvin's little space into a weeded, weekend paradise. By the time the sun had set, we were fresh out of spaces, with more money in our pockets than the people inside The Fair had. Days like this hadn't come around too often for us out there.

No, we didn't cure cancer, or solve world peace, or really do much of anything in the grand scheme, but we had ourselves a day, and that meant everything to us. On a day where everyone we interacted with was *spending* money, we were the ones *making* it!

We were *finally* the ones making the money.

And even though we were still home less, we were able to "keep the lights on" yet another day.

So, we celebrated with fried chicken. All 4 of us sat around a big bucket at this nearby shack and dug in as it poured. The rain on our faces might as well have been tears of joy. We didn't say much, our smiles spoke for us. We knew Saturday and Sunday would be even busier. We'd found a hustle and built something, a trend we hoped would spill over into the rest of our somewhat uninspiring lives. We were probably going to be millionaires, we figured.

All was right with the world, and that bird didn't stand a chance. I slept damn good that night on the Big Red Couch. We might've even fallen asleep with the lights on.

The next morning, we woke up early and made a sign. Because that's what people with money do. *"$20 for PARKING,"* it read... or something, and we headed back to paradise.

When we got there, our jaws dropped. All hell had broken loose. Our lot had been roped off. Not by the police, but rather some dude claiming that *he* actually owned the lot, not us. Spray painted lines, orange-ass cones, and a far more extravagant sign than ours, all accompanied by a man sitting in a chair with a water bottle, and a damned umbrella hat.

Confused and disappointed aren't nearly strong enough words. So, we called Mr. Calvin.

According to Mr. Calvin, he'd sold the land to this guy many years ago. "I didn't want to tell you boys that, because I wanted you to win. I'm sorry. I'll come pick y'all up." It was never ours to begin with? I suppose all is fair at the Fair, but this sucked.

Talk about a quiet ride. We hadn't brought in what we thought we'd make, but we did *bring in*. And it was much more than we had when the weekend started, so ultimately, we were thankful. Melancholy, but thankful.

Before we got out of the car, we were splitting up the cash to give Mr. Calvin his share of our earnings when he turned around with a smile: "Don't worry about it boys, you done good out there. Sometimes it's better to not know nothin' than to know too much. Sometimes, the early bird gets the worm. Sometimes ain't no worm. Save your lil' money for a burger and a beer."

We'd gotten lucky one last time. Thank God. Like I said, it wasn't much, but that pocket change came with some perspective, a hot and crispy box of bird, and some of the brightest lights I'd ever seen.

By the time The Fair would come again the next year, I'd be long gone. But, the lessons from that day still stick with me.

For starters, competition on the open market is fierce, and sometimes there really are no rules to this shit. Just get started. You'll figure out the rest.

Next, the early bird really does get the worm - it's a business baby.

Also, every so often, it's okay to dance in the rain and get a little wet.

And finally, when the Fair is in town, everyone is trying to keep the lights on.

"But I will not lose, for even in defeat there's a valuable lesson learned, so it evens it up for me." — Jay-Z

"..SOMETIMES THE EARLY BIRD GETS THE WORM. SOMETIMES AIN'T NO WORM."

Would You Like Half
of My Sandwich?

...because I'd like half of yours

I'm not gonna say I was asleep, but I damn sure wasn't up. Awake? Sure. Alert? Sorta. Tired? Absolutely.

I'd been running around Dallas all day trying to keep the lights on, and this particular good day ended with me riding the DART train at sunset, searching desperately for some shut-eye.

It was all a dream, really. For real though, it was. I was dreaming about condiments, toasted bread, toppings, meat, and cheese. Weird shit, I'm aware.

I'd fallen asleep with the second half of a sandwich in my hand. The plan was to save some for later, but unbeknownst to me at the time, I'd already taken my last bite.

This all started because one of the cats I knew out there, a photographer, needed some help with a job, and it was raining. So, I told him I could hold an umbrella, keep shit dry, or do whatever for him, for as long as he needed me to do it, in exchange for $50 and lunch. What a tough bargain I drove. He agreed and off we went.

Now, me and this guy knew each other, for sure ...even if we didn't *know* each other, you know? Like, I knew his first and last name (but not his middle), his favorite sport (but not his favorite team or athlete), how many siblings he had (but not their names or ages). I even knew that he was from Dallas, but I had no clue as to what part of the city... that sort of thing.

That would soon change, though, because I was about to have half of his sandwich.

The morning had flown by, we'd gotten some good pictures, and it was time to eat.

"My momma always said you can learn a lot about a person by the way they make their sandwich."

Yep, just like that. It wasn't ceremonious, epic, or profound, or anything like that. He just sort of...said it—I'm not even sure he knew I heard him. As a matter of fact, as soon as we walked into that Subway for lunch, he had a plan. I watched him make his sandwich: white bread, turkey, jalapeños toasted under the Swiss cheese, banana peppers, salt and pepper, and more. It was an orchestra!

As for me, to be honest, I was just there for a quick and easy tuna sub, but after seeing his display, I ended up getting banana peppers and jalapeños too! I suppose there's a first time for everything, and since he did it, I did it.

Next thing you know, we were sitting down chatting. We talked about family, relationships, music, religion, college days, career dreams, and more. I even found out his middle name. And it went both ways — he learned a good bit about me too, of which I was happy to share, in fact.

Then, I thought about how crazy it was that we'd spent so many weeks up to that point sharing that Big Red Couch (and that tiny ass blanket), an occasional burger and beer, sold parking spots at The Fair together, and somehow, sort of barely even knew each other.

I think that's what made the chat so comforting — the sanctity of sharing a meal and a conversation with someone you want to know more about. Maybe it was the idea that by learning more about someone else, I could learn more about myself? Or maybe I was just happy to be making some cold hard cash, and eating good for a change.

As we were wrapping up lunch, I decided to save the final six inches of my tuna for later. I knew the sandwich would come in handy at some point, and when we broke at the end of the day, it did.

I headed to that train ride I was telling you about earlier.

Where was I? Oh yeah.

So, I'm not gonna say I was asleep, but I damn sure wasn't up. But sitting there, eyes closed, with my sandwich clenched tight, I was at least half awake. I'd had enough money to actually buy a train ticket this time, which meant no cops to keep an eye peeled for, so I didn't have a care in the world (generally speaking). I deserved this!

And just before I was about to doze off, something hit me:

If you can learn a lot about a person from talking to them...and if you can learn a lot about a man by the way he makes his sandwich...then could we all... "be"...sandwiches ourselves?

Well, maybe not a literal sandwich itself, but perhaps the ingredients that make them up? The family, the hobbies, career paths, the music or religion choices, and other quirks of each other we'd been exchanging all day. Maybe they were just the bread, meat, cheese, toppings and condiments of our own sandwiches! The elements that make us awesome and unique.

This was some trippy shit, but there was still something there—dream or no dream. And that *something* left me searching for the connective thread between these sandwiches, our interactions, and the "ingredients" therein.

Sharing your "sandwich" with someone, I realized, is primarily a petition to grow closer. It's a hell of a gesture to offer up your attention, time, and self to someone else. Sharing a sandwich is vulnerable, but it can be fun too. Because a lot of times, if I offer my half to you, I'm hoping you'll do the same for me—that way we can both enjoy BOTH.

If I offer you half of my sandwich, it's not only because I want you to know more about me, but because I want to learn more about you, too. Humans are sort of selfish; let's be honest. And whether you're consciously or subconsciously looking to benefit yourself, offering up half of your sandwich is a great start. You can't lose.

So yeah, you *can* learn a lot about a person by the way they make their sandwich.

Nowadays, I offer half of my sandwich all the time. I've used this Sandwich Method to package myself when I meet people at parties, go on dates, and even in job interviews. From family and coworkers, to new acquaintances, be like a sandwich, my friend.

It's helped me better package and understand myself. People offer you half of their sandwich not because you look hungry, or they assumed you forgot your lunch. It's not because they want to gloat about how tasty jalapeños and banana peppers are together, either. And it's definitely not because they don't want to finish it...

I'm offering you half of my sandwich because I want half of yours!

By the time I woke, I'd almost missed my stop. As I was walking toward the door, I looked down at that tuna sub, and all of a sudden knew exactly where it belonged. I gave it to this homeless man toward the front of the train. I'd seen him when I first got on, and I could tell he wouldn't be getting off until somebody made him get off. I'd been there in his shoes on many a different day, and mostly, all I remembered was being hungry as hell.

And that's one last thing about being home less. There are many times you find that you actually have a lot to give.

So I walked up to him and asked, *"Would you like half of my sand...?*

AND THAT'S ONE LAST THING ABOUT BEING HOME LESS. THERE ARE MANY TIMES YOU FIND THAT YOU ACTUALLY HAVE A LOT TO GIVE.

SO I WALKED UP TO HIM AND ASKED, *"WOULD YOU LIKE HALF OF MY SAND...?"*

IOME LESS IN DALLAS

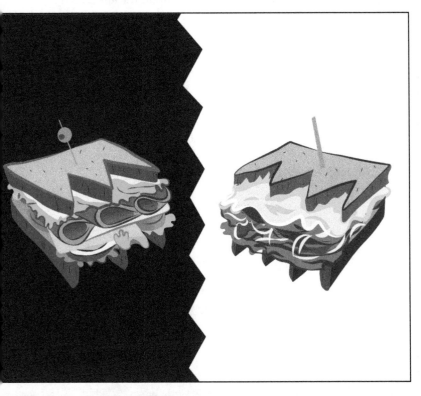

A word from Blake

The paradox about a moment in time is that its impact can last forever. The lessons from past experiences become a guiding light toward the future. Troy candidly describes what it's like being home less in Dallas and the life-lessons learned from it.

And if you don't know, now you know.

I know, because I was right there with him. When the whole crew sat around the table and decided to bet the house on ourselves (before we even had a house to bet), it could've been a scene right out of a movie. We chose to chase a dream, no matter what it cost, and in the process, friends became family. Chasing dreams can be expensive, but the friendships and lessons that last a lifetime? Priceless...or whatever Mastercard and them said.

I hope you enjoyed this collection of stories, as it is an example of Troy's special ability to bring light to any situation, regardless of circumstance. Nine years later, Troy is still one of my closest friends. We often reminisce about the good times and laugh at the struggles.

Never forget to enjoy the burger while it's hot, and the beer while it's cold.

To my brother from another, Cheers!

BLAKE ROBERTS
Marketing Strategist, Friend

Acknowledgments

They say it takes a village to raise a child. But who knew making this book would too?!

Thank you to *Rai Robledo* (layout and cover designer), *Xavier Payne* (illustrator), *Nya B* (audiobook producer), *Lincoln Stephens* and *Blake Roberts* (for their personal words at the beginning and end of this thing, respectively), *Laura Relyea* (for making things make a lot of sense toward the end), *my family* (for always having my back—especially my mom for being a good sport about that skit in there), *Sam Floyd* (my Grits & Gospel co-founder, writing partner, primary editor, and best friend all these years), *Renita Bryant* (the first person that thought to publish our work), and *Paige* (who is the best at telling me when my stuff is good and, more importantly, when it still needs some work).

Also, to the city of Dallas: forever a second home to me.

Printed in the USA
CPSIA information can be obtained
at www.ICGtesting.com
JSHW061933300723
45168JS00001BA/11

9 781957 092669